A CONFIDENT ME

A BLACK GIRL'S GUIDE TO FINDING HER INNER CONFIDENCE

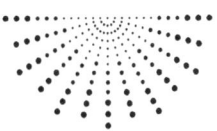

MELODIE WILLIAMS

Copyright © 2020 by Melodie Williams

All rights reserved.

Published by Firebrand Publishing Atlanta, GA USA

No part of this book may be reproduced in any form or by any electronic or mechanical means, including information storage and retrieval systems, without written permission from the author, except for the use of brief quotations in a book review and certain other noncommercial uses permitted by copyright law.

For permission requests, write to the publisher, addressed "Attention: Permissions coordinator," at the email address: support@firebrandpublishing.com

Limit of Liability/Disclaimer of Warranty: While the publisher and author have used their best efforts in preparing this book, they make no representations or warranties with respect to the accuracy or completeness of the contents of this book and specifically disclaim any implied warranties of merchantability or fitness for a particular purpose. No warranty may be created or extended by sales representatives or written sales materials. The advice and strategies contained herein may not be suitable for your situation. You should consult with a professional where appropriate. Neither the publisher nor the author shall be liable for damages arising here from.

Firebrand Publishing publishes in a variety of print and

electronic formats and by print-on-demand. For more information about Firebrand Publishing products, visit https://firebrandpublishing.com

Book Cover Designer: Arvelle Jamal

ISBN: 978-1-941907-17-7 (paperback)

ISBN: 978-1-941907-16-0 (ebook)

Printed in the United States of America

To Madison, Maliyah, Savannah, and Maghen David

To: Alexia Michelle and Mykayla Marie

To: Channel for encouraging me more than you'll ever know

CONTENTS

Foreword	ix
Introduction	xi
1. Self Love	1
Notes	15
2. Exclusion	17
Notes	31
3. Kindness & Conflict	33
Notes	49
4. Value	51
Notes	69
Glossary	71
About the Author	77

FOREWORD

I used to wonder how it felt, to live in that kind of freedom where you didn't have to fight, or constantly watch your back or wonder if your rejection had to do with your actual shortcomings or the color of your skin, and the stereotypes that come with it.

But then I started to feel bad for them. In my struggle, my strength is displayed. My fight, my ability to break glass ceilings, my resilience all make me proud to be in this battle.

The fact that I'm part of a group of people that are looked at as least, but have proven

FOREWORD

time and time again, since the beginning of creation, that they are actually the greatest, makes me feel so honored to be on this side.

And then I feel sad for them.

Sad that they just get it easy and I get to fight and find out who I really am, how powerful my presence is and what I'm really made of.

INTRODUCTION

Let's face it, the world doesn't go easy on girls of color. However, there are steps we can take to ensure we stand tall, no matter what.

Walk with me as we focus in on a few key ways to build your confidence and allow that new found confidence to shine through you.

Tips:

- Take your time
- Apply what you learn
- Any single **bolded** word or name

INTRODUCTION

you come across can be found in the glossary at the back of this book.

Enjoy!

-*Melodie*

1
SELF LOVE

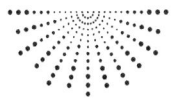

Self-Love: The celebration, appreciation, and acceptance of one's self

I LOVE ME BECAUSE...

I KNOW WHAT YOU'RE THINKING. THAT'S quite a strong statement to start out with right? I mean sure, there are special days designated to celebrate our parents, grandparents, or other parental figures where we write meaningful letters and poems (or we find cards that say exactly how we feel), there's even a day designated for us to tell our friends and significant others how we feel about them, but there's not really a day that tells us to express why we love ourselves.

All of the major codes of conduct that are taught to us when we first enter school encourage a love for others (i.e. share, be kind, treat others how you want to be treated, etc.), but there aren't many codes or rules that encourage us to love ourselves just as we are.

A lot of times, saying "I love me" even without the 'because' indicates a form of selfishness or arrogance (to some people).

But why shouldn't we take the time to express why or what we love about ourselves? Maybe not at a podium in front of your entire school, but to ourselves. After all, we're not trying to convince people that we love ourselves. We're actually establishing to ourselves why we love our self. I know that was a lot of 'self' used there, but that's why this chapter is called 'Self-Love' so keep up.

Why is the issue of self-love so important?

Well I'm so glad you asked!

Thing is, we can't expect others to truly love us, when we don't even love ourselves.

Wait, hold on let's back up a second. Realistically, your parents and other family members will probably always genuinely love you. Your mother birthed you and had an unexplainable love for you even while you were growing in her womb. Maybe you have a mother whose womb you didn't grow in, maybe your mother had a desire to be a mom so she sought you out, or maybe a family member is taking the place of your mom. Regardless of who your actual 'mother' is, that person was given an extra dose of care just for you and even at your very worst, she will generally still love you.

Now, back to the matter at hand. We can't expect even our closest friends to truly love us as we are, when we do not love nor have we accepted ourselves. As much as you guys hang out, text, and swap stories over the phone they can't love the 'true you' when you haven't accepted the 'true you'. They may really like who you're pretending to be, or the false impression you've given, but not the 'true you'.

When we don't allow people to see who we truly are, we not only cheat ourselves, but we cheat our friends out of the opportunity to know and love someone great.

Why else?

Because in the Bible, Psalm 139:13 says, "For You [God] formed my inward parts, You [God] knitted me together in my mother's womb" (**ESV**).

This bible verse simply tells us that God took the time to make us and secure us in our mother's wombs so that we can be here today. If God loved me that much I should no doubt love myself. The next verse in that same bible chapter goes on to say, "Thank You for making me so wonderfully complex! Your **workmanship** is marvelous – how well I know it." (v. 14 **NLT**)

Yo! God used His workmanship to make me wonderfully complex! Despite what the world says you should be, or your classmates, your friends, or even your family members, God made you who you are and trust me that was no accident.

I don't know about you, but that's enough to at least make me explore the option of indulging in some self-love.

THE FACT OF THE MATTER IS, LIFE IS A whole lot better when you love yourself. Life's basic rules that encourage love for one another, mean nothing if you do not love yourself.

It's simply that, I can't genuinely love you, if I don't love me.

I can't genuinely encourage my friends when they're down or having relationship troubles (trust me, the time will come and they'll need you), I can't defend them, I can't forgive them, and I can't accept them because I haven't accepted myself.

Quite frankly, until we tackle self-love no other part in this book will matter.

Now that we've established the 'why' let's get into the 'how.'

You see, society doesn't make it easy for young girls of color to love themselves. The 'image' of beauty set forth may not be the image you see when you look in the mirror. Between that and the **stereotypes**, it's pretty easy to not see your worth or value (something we'll also talk about later). But forget what society says! Forget what everyone else likes! What do you like?

From the time I was in about 4th grade all the way through high school, everyone always made comments about the size of my forehead. As a matter of fact, it was known as a 'five-head' (which is actually pretty funny when I think about it). There was a girl in my high school who would literally tap me on my forehead every time she saw me. Her intent wasn't to bully me (annoy me maybe), she just thought it was so funny that my forehead was big. You know what's crazy? I never saw anything wrong with my forehead. Sure it was big, but I thought it fit me. I seriously felt like it flowed with my whole look. I never wore bangs to hide it or any other concealing hairstyle. I've actually always preferred styles with my hair pulled up.

It's not that self-love is just about the outer appearance, but we all like to be pleased with our outer appearance and that's okay because remember, God used his workmanship to make us complex.

Your skin, your lips, your hair, your body shape, all those things make up 'you'.

. . .

MELODIE WILLIAMS

What do you see that you like?

What do you see that you don't like?

I once heard a little girl say she didn't play outside during the summer because she didn't want her skin to get any darker. It broke my heart. She had the most beautiful skin and she was literally robbing herself of her childhood because somewhere in life she picked up the idea that there was such a thing as 'too dark'.

In an article written by Kate Smith, the color brown is defined as stability, reliability, and approachability. It's associated with things that are natural and organic. In other words, there is absolutely nothing wrong with it, no matter the shade.

There is beauty in everything. Beauty doesn't reside in a certain body weight, skin shade, or hair texture. Own your beauty!

Plus, everything's better with a dose of confidence.

IF YOU ARE STRUGGLING TO SEE YOUR outer beauty, I won't deceive you into thinking you'll begin to see it overnight. If you've already been suckered into the world's standard of beauty, you'll need to deprogram yourself.

Take some time and write down what you like about yourself. This may be tough, but on the same page write down what you don't like and next to your 'dislike' write something good about that feature. If you can't think of anything at all, just write 'God gave it to me.'

Hey, don't be afraid to ask God to help you see your beauty, after all, He gave it to you!

NOW LET'S GO IN DEEPER.

Who are you?

MELODIE WILLIAMS

What do you like?

What are you good at?

Owning and accepting the answers to all those questions contribute to self-love.

Before you say it, we are all good at something. You may not sing and dance like Beyoncé or flip like Gabby and Simone or run like **Flo Jo**, my bad, I mean Allyson Felix, but you are good at something.

You may be a good teacher like **Marva Collins**. You may be excellent at leading others like **Ella Baker**. You may be a great writer like **Zora Neale Hurston**. These may not be names we hear often (anymore), but nonetheless these women of color knew what they were good at and ran with it. If you find something you really love, but aren't confident in your abilities, work at it. When you improve and succeed you will have a better appreciation for yourself.

More Than Just a Pretty Face

A CONFIDENT ME

Yes, you. You are more than just a pretty face. Some of you may not struggle with seeing your outer beauty, which is great. However, please know you are more than just a pretty face. You have some sort of gift or talent that will get you further in life than your looks will ever get you. Don't let anyone tell you different.

Let's address the question of 'who you are.'

If we don't accept who we are, we will believe anything someone says about us. If you are a Black American born in the United States, more than likely your ancestors were brought here during the **Transatlantic Slave Trade**. The Transatlantic Slave Trade, one of the greatest atrocities that ever took place, was the process of taking Africans from West African countries to the Caribbean and the Americas to enslave them. Africans were densely packed on ships like cargo. The space provided for each individual, no matter their size was about 5 feet 6 inches (keep in mind most males are about 5 feet 10 inches). During the journey some died, but many survived. Some even tried killing themselves, but were unsuccessful, thus surviving. They went on to face 200 years of slavery. No, not **Indentured Servants**, but slaves. They worked all year around, sun up to sun down. The women gave birth, and were back out in the fields the same week. Working under extreme conditions were not fed very well, were not paid (of course) but they survived. The women were raped and beaten, yet they survived. You are here today, because they survived. You are a descendant of those who survived. You are a descendant of those who went on to become doctors, lawyers, writers, inventors, educators, and leaders. You descended from all out survivors. Be proud of that! Let that encourage you. Strive to learn more about them and the names mentioned earlier. Having a sense of who you are, is a major contributor to self-love.

Wherever your family is from, do some

research and find out about your ancestors. They played a major part in who you are today.

Since self-love is the celebration, acceptance, and appreciation of one's self, let's try this:

I celebrate me because...

Give it some thought and visit the mirror each morning with a new reason why you celebrate yourself.

NOTES

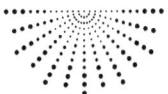

2
EXCLUSION

Exclusion: Set apart; denied access

"Yes Granny, Honors English is no joke," Lauren yelled over the rattling of dishes to her grandmother. "We really had to buckle down to put some serious study time in."

Lauren's grandmother came to stay the weekend to care for her younger siblings while Mr. Gavis, Lauren's father, went on a three-day business trip.

Although Lauren had been very convincing about her dedication to studying for finals, she and her friend Kyndal, who was also staying over for the weekend, actually had not been studying at all.

See, the night before, when Lauren was sure her father was safely in flight, she told her grandmother that Kyndal would be over for the weekend to prepare for finals week (that's actually the same story she told Kyndal). Lauren, however, had another plan. Her father had recently purchased a brand new SUV and his little red Honda had been sitting collecting dust in the driveway for quite some time. Lauren figured this was her shot. She may have only been 13, but her older cousin taught her how to drive years ago and she was ready. There seemed to be no better time than this.

How would she do it? How would she possibly be able to leave the house for hours on end without her grandmother knowing? Furthermore, if a whole automobile has been sitting in the same place for months, why wouldn't anyone notice it suddenly being gone? These were **adequate** inquiries, at least Kyndal thought so. Oh but Lauren. Lauren knew her grandmother very well. That evening, when her father left, she told her grandmother they had some serious studying to do. "We'll be locked in this room Granny," Lauren said. "We ate already. Can you just leave the laundry basket by the door?" Lauren humbly asked. "I'll make sure to get it."

"Also, can you make sure the kids don't bother us? I really need to get a good grade," Lauren pleaded as her grandmother honored each request. "How is this working?" Kyndal thought to herself. "This will never work." Oh, but it did.

What started out as a simple joy ride around the block turned into an excursion throughout all the nearby cities. Lauren was on a high. Kyndal, not so much. The first hour Kyndal was able to convince herself that this was all harmless fun, but the 'fun' just never seemed to end. The very things that terrified Kyndal, the 'almost' accident, nearly being caught by a neighborhood parent, and just about running out of gas were the very things that fueled Lauren's excitement. Thankfully after three and a half long hours it was finally over. The girls managed to sneak back into the house, pull that laundry basket in the room, and quietly go to sleep as if nothing happened. "At least it's over," Kyndal thought.

Thought was right. The following afternoon just as Lauren finished convincing her grandmother that they really 'buckled down,' she grabbed the landline phone out of the kitchen wall to call Reagan. Reagan was another friend from school, who although may not have had the adventurous ideas, was always down for the cause. Lauren filled Reagan in on all the highs of the previous night (with a bit of embellishment of course) and convinced her she had to come by and get in on all the fun.

A CONFIDENT ME

"The fun?" Kyndal thought. She had assumed it was all over.

The adventure was far from over. A new plan had just been set in place. This time, Lauren was going to move her dad's car about halfway down the block while her grandmother was occupied in the kitchen. The new story-line was that Reagan's brother was going to come and pick them up and drop them off at the mall. "We would've asked you Granny," Lauren said sweetly, "but I didn't want you to have to pack up the kids." This girl was good!

After Kyndal's silent prayers didn't seem to be working, her only hope was for Reagan to back out. "Yea, maybe she won't show," Kyndal hoped. Wrong. Reagan already agreed to have her brother drop her off in the same spot down the block where the Honda was parked. The plan was gold. At this point, a more than worried Kyndal could no longer hold it in. "Let's not do it," she said to Lauren. "We can just stay in and chill, we don't have much money anyway," Kyndal urged. Wrong again. Lauren's grandmother placed two crisp $20 bills on the kitchen counter for the mall trip. Kyndal then tried coming up with every excuse why it would be better to just stay in, even listing all possible dangers and potential trouble, and nothing seemed to work. As a matter of fact, the more Kyndal fought against the idea the more annoyed Lauren got. Not to mention Reagan's brother's car could now be seen coming up the street. It was a wrap. She couldn't stay at the house (at least she didn't think that would be a wise option), so along she went.

With Reagan cheering Lauren on, it seemed as if the evening would never end. With more encouragement, came more boldness. These three 13 year olds were now cruising down the highway headed into the big city. This was unreal. Last night's uneasiness was literally a walk in the park compared to the terror Kyndal now felt and every moment Kyndal wasn't having a good time fed Lauren's fury with her. But at last the night came to an end.

Although everyone made it home safely and no one snitched and the 'vehicle to freedom' made its way back to its home in the driveway school on Monday was somehow different.

Kyndal knew Lauren had been irritated with her over the weekend, but everything was cool now, right? Well, let me tell you, just as crafty as Lauren was in convincing her grandmother that she would be in all night studying, she somehow used that same bit of intelligence to turn Reagan and now Shannon, who did not even partake in the adventure, against Kyndal.

What started out as an avoidance of conversation turned into mall trips, sleepovers, and 3-way conference calls with the exception of one. Kyndal was excluded.

I WISH I COULD TELL YOU THAT everyone got over themselves and became the best of friends living happily ever after, but then again that wouldn't even be realistic.

Kyndal was excluded. She was denied access. There were days when she was invited to 'belong' in the group, but if there was ever a desire to leave someone out Kyndal was the perfect person. 'Kyndal' also just so happens to be the author of this book.

IT WAS EASY FOR ME TO BELIEVE THAT expressing that I did not want to engage in car theft (hey let's just call it what it was) was the reason for me being denied access. I wished I had never gone to sleep over that weekend, or that I was just a whole lot more chill during the illegal act. With all that, the truth is, I would've been excluded anyway. Exclusion happens and I was the prime target.

ALIENATION OR EXCLUSION TYPICALLY occurs when a group of people deny access to another person based on their looks, beliefs, or social class. This is something we see quite a bit of in life.

I looked different, my values were different, and my actions were different. Them excluding me was practically a no brainer.

Now, I'm not saying that you will always be excluded if you're different, but I am saying it happens. It is a part of life. In fact, not long ago, I was excluded by some young ladies at work. Crazy right? Here I am, a full grown adult, being alienated at my own job.

Excluded. Denied access. You may be reading this and have already faced exclusion where your access was denied to a certain group of people or maybe even a set of activities. Do not fret, you are not alone.

Exclusion and alienation take place in all parts of the world and has been going on since the beginning of time.

White American women were excluded from voting in political elections all the way until 1920. Black American women (and men) were excluded all the way up until 1965. Black

Americans were also excluded from certain schools, using certain restrooms, eating in certain restaurants, gaining knowledge from certain books, and many other things. The point is, exclusion is something we will all face and there are no set of rules to follow to avoid it.

Someone else's acceptance or inclusion of you does not define who you are. Nor does it increase (or decrease) your value (that word again).

Now let's talk about the other part of exclusion, being set apart. Being set apart takes place when we exclude ourselves. Wait, so in a world filled with exclusion and alienation, there are times when we should exclude ourselves? Absolutely!

In the previous chapter, we talked about self-love. When we truly love ourselves there are just certain things we refuse to indulge in and in turn have to set ourselves apart.

The previous questions asked were, "what

do you like?" and "what are you good at?" Now the question is:

What do you stand for?

WHAT WOULD YOU LIKE TO BE known for?

IF YOU STAND FOR KINDNESS AND WOULD like to be known as someone who is kind and trustworthy, it would be a great idea to steer clear of things that go against kindness and trustworthiness.

That means if the whole school has banned together against one person (or maybe just a group of girls at the lunch table), you set yourself apart and be the kind girl you have committed to being.

If you stand for leadership and would like to influence others, you should make an effort to reach out and help others and set yourself apart from things that tear others down. Even if it's the **Status Quo**.

IT WILL NOT ALWAYS BE EASY, BUT IT will certainly be worth it. When you stand true to what you believe, others will stop asking you to do things that go against your beliefs. You will become known for what you stand for and commit to. Your true commitment to something will cause others to respect you.

Setting yourself apart can also ease the hurt of being excluded or denied access by others.

Recap:

- Exclusion or being denied access is a part of life.
- Making a decision about who we are and what we stand for causes us to exclude ourselves or be set apart.

Take some time to answer these questions:

- What do you stand for?
- What would you like to be known for?

NOTES

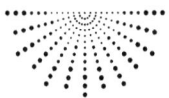

3
KINDNESS & CONFLICT

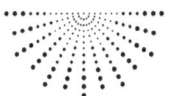

Kindness: The act of being friendly, encouraging, considerate and loving

Conflict: A dispute, disagreement, or misunderstanding

W E STARTED OUT TALKING ABOUT SELF-love because it's hard to show kindness to others when we are unhappy with ourselves. It is vital for us to understand that often people are rude to us, or may take *'shots'* at us, and even *'throw shade'* because they are unhappy with themselves. They may even be facing pain they aren't ready to talk about yet.

Now, this doesn't make their acts of 'un' kindness permissible, but understanding this can help us have a little more patience with them, while also helping us not take things so personal.

Projection

Have you ever seen a projection screen? Back in my day, we frequently used **projectors** and projection screens in school. We usually took notes based on what was presented on the projection screen. With all the technology upgrades over a couple of decades (yes, decades), projectors and projection screens work a little differently, but the end goal is still the same.

A projector uses a lens, lights, and a mirror to display a picture (still image, movies, or even a slide show presentation) on a screen. A projection screen.

A CONFIDENT ME

Myla needed to conquer the most challenging task she ever encountered. She needed to transition into doing her own hair. Myla went to the beauty shop for years, but with her mom starting a new job that required her to work most weekends, that was no longer possible. There was no longer time for a long day in the salon when, in the words of her mother, "you should be trying to learn your own hair anyway."

So that's just what she did, or at least attempted to do. Myla logged on to the *'School of YouTube'* to learn different hair styles and techniques. Never having had her hair relaxed, and usually only having to create a style after her hair had been stretched, she was in for quite a challenge. This was a challenge Myla was up for, as she twisted her hair up at night and arose earlier than normal to ensure satisfaction.

What started out as a duel between Myla and her own God-given natural hair turned into a beautiful friendship, as she learned her hair's likes and dislikes. Myla was proud of her new found relationship. There were some rough mornings, but all in all, she was excited about her new skill. Not only was she creating pretty cool hairstyles (although the results were quite different from her new YouTube instructors), she was experiencing a new kind of freedom coupled with a feeling of accomplishment.

However, not everyone was receptive to the 'New Myla.' Sure she got the usual, "cute hair!" and "I see you, girl!" in the hallways at school from a few friends, but no matter what, Brooke always had a snide remark... And I mean, no matter what.

This was a new journey for Myla but even if she left her house feeling *bomb*, an interaction with Brooke always left her feeling knocked down a few pegs.

Brooke knew just what to say to get under Myla's skin. If it wasn't the size or texture of her afro that day, it was the way she parted it or the structure of her bun. Oh, and don't let

A CONFIDENT ME

Myla try something new like two French braids, it was over, the mean comments would never end!

Brooke seemed to target a lot of the things Myla was feeling unsure about on her new journey. It didn't stop Myla from trying, but it definitely made this new journey a lot more difficult than it ever needed to be.

So who is this girl who seemed to know everything about hair?

Someone who knew nothing about hair!

Brooke generally wore braids paired with a scarf or headband worn at the perimeter of her head (she basically covered her edges). Very rarely was she seen without braids. On occasion she would rock a tight low bun, but never was she seen without a headband or scarf.

Well, it turns out, Miss Brooke had her own hair issues. She had a family member who braided her hair, just not often enough. She really didn't have the slightest clue how to manage her own hair, nor did she try. The scarves and headbands were not so much a style, but a means of hiding her edges. The very girl who had so much to say about someone else's hair, had the nerve to be insecure about her own.

Brooke didn't like the way her hair looked without braids, nor did she like the way her edges looked when her braids grew out and got loose. Her resolve? Always keep them covered. In her mind, she wouldn't be drawing attention to them.

Brooke was secretly bothered that she couldn't manage her own hair. It drove her crazy inside seeing Myla's new found confidence, and that Myla was able to create new styles. She hated that Myla was consistently getting better all by herself, by simply trying and watching videos on YouTube.

Projection. Brooke was projecting her uncertainties and insecurities onto Myla. Brooke is the projector. Her negative thoughts and insecurities are the lens and lights. Her reflection of herself is the mirror and Myla was her projection screen.

Rather than Brooke dealing with her own insecurities (which she may not have fully realized she had), or asking for help, OR just being happy for another girl trying something new and succeeding, she projected her insecurities onto Myla. Brooke became a *'hater'* and tried really hard to make Myla feel unsure about herself because of her own uncertainties.

THIS STORY FALLS INTO OUR KINDNESS and Conflict chapter because as we begin to understand projection, we will stop allowing ourselves to be a participant in every argument or *'beef'* we are invited to attend. When we know who we are, and love who we are, we won't be so easily moved when people purposely try to tear us down. We will understand that the conflict they are brewing, contains ingredients of their own insecurities and lack of **self-worth,** and has nothing to do with us.

CONFLICT

Now let's talk about conflict. Conflict, much like exclusion, is inevitable. You could potentially experience conflict in every type of relationship you have. Although that may seem troubling, resolving conflict helps relationships grow stronger, and allows you to get to know people better.

Notice I said *resolving* conflict.

Now, all conflict won't be the same, but rest assured the person you are conflicting with just wants to be heard. The most important thing to do when you are faced with conflict in your relationship is to hear each other out. Most conflicts occur because of misunderstandings. Seek to understand one another. Try to see the other person's point of view even when you don't agree with it. If you hurt someone, apologize even if hurting them wasn't your intent. Remember, the apology is for hurt feelings and to resolve the conflict.

KINDNESS

You see, we couldn't start out with kindness the way our general codes of conduct do when we enter the world. As stated previously, if we don't love and accept who we are (flaws and all) we have nothing to give.

Brooke didn't love who she was and was struggling with the very thing Myla was succeeding at. This made it impossible for her to extend kindness.

THE TRUTH ABOUT KINDNESS

Even when you have loved and accepted yourself, it is still challenging to be kind. Being truly committed to being a kind girl requires work. I won't even let you believe it's easy, because it is not. There will be times when you will need to go above and beyond for someone and let's be real, that can be **grueling**. But guess what? It'll be worth it.

Would you believe the largest missing **aspect** among women is kindness?

We talked about exclusion (not kind). We talked about projecting insecurities onto someone, which is basically being a hater (also not kind), so it's probably not too surprising that being unkind or mean, is so **prevalent** among women and girls alike.

Once again, this is why we tackled self-love first. I can't stress this enough, we cannot honestly love someone and show genuine kindness, when we don't love ourselves first. It's like pouring from an empty cup.

Imagine having a tall glass on a hot sunny day. Your best friend sees you and she is panting hard because the beaming hot sun has driven her into exhaustion. She sees your tall glass dripping beads of condensation, and her eyes get big, because she has been waiting for something to quench her thirst.

She comes up to you and asks for just a waterfall, and you agree. So she tilts her head back, and you lift your glass up and turn it to give her, her life changing waterfall into her **parched** mouth and nothing comes out. Your glass is completely empty. Your BFF is literally dying of thirst and you have nothing to give her and more importantly, you have nothing to give yourself.

That is what it's like to try being loving and kind to someone, when you do not love yourself. This can probably explain the lack of kindness seen amongst women and girls.

You can't show love and kindness and be encouraging and accepting if you haven't taken the time to love and accept yourself.

I know that is a bit of a recap from our '**Self-Love' chapter**, but it's really important that we grasp that before diving into what it looks like to love others.

. . .

So what does kindness look like?

The greatest thing about kindness is that so many different actions fall under the umbrella of kindness.

- **Thoughtfulness**
- **Friendliness**
- **Encouragement**
- **Patience**
- **Compassion**
- **Generosity**
- **Loyalty**
- **Empathy**

To name a few.

Let's take encouragement for instance. Encouraging someone is an act of kindness. Remember Brooke and Myla? What if Brooke had just told Myla she was doing a good job with her hair? What if she had simply turned all her negative comments about Myla's hair into positive ones? What if rather than tearing Myla down, Brooke encouraged her? In doing so, Brooke might have even solved her own problem.

We don't know what someone is facing and we don't know how much easier we can make it or how we can brighten up their day by simply encouraging them. You see someone working hard? Tell them "good job" you see their hard work and encourage them to keep pushing. You see someone succeeding at something after not doing so well? Tell them good job and encourage them to stay consistent. You can find a way to encourage someone in anything!

Encouragement can even come in the form of compliments. You see a girl with nice style or cool hair, tell her! Don't you feel good when someone compliments you? Allow another girl to experience that same feeling.

Encourage other girls. Encourage your friends, it takes nothing from you. It's important to keep your friends encouraged, we need each other.

We'll grab a couple more from our list.

Let's talk about loyalty.

What does it look like when you are a loyal person?

When you're loyal, you are the girl you are committed to being. If you committed to being friends with someone then you'll be a good friend to them even when it's hard. If someone tells you something in confidence and asks you not to tell anyone, being loyal means you keep that information to yourself. Being loyal is defending your friend when others are tarnishing her name in your presence (whether they are speaking truths or not). Being loyal is committed to doing what you set out to do. Be it a project, a team you've joined, or even just helping someone out in need. Being a loyal girl means doing what you said you would do.

WHAT ABOUT COMPASSION?

What does compassion look like?

Being compassionate means showing care and concern for someone. You ever see another girl having a bad day? Showing compassion could be just asking if everything is alright. If you see another girl in need, showing compassion is finding out what she needs and meeting that need.

RECAP:

- Remember to be a listening ear when being faced with conflict.
- It's important to keep your friends encouraged, we need each other.
- You never know what your act of kindness can do for the next girl.

NOTES

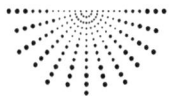

4
VALUE

Value: To hold something in high regard; the importance or worth of something

EVERY CHAPTER WE GO INTO IS BUILT ON the foundation of self-love. Without first talking about self-love it would be as if we were building a house on sinking sand. We need a nice strong foundation to build on.

. . .

So let's do a brief rundown:

- *Because we love ourselves we understand that we will be excluded.*

- *Because we love ourselves we understand that sometimes we have to exclude ourselves, or set ourselves apart in order to stay committed to who we are.*

- *Because we love and accept ourselves we can genuinely love and accept others and be kind to one another.*

- *We can now handle conflict correctly by listening and being open minded.*

- *We also know how to walk away from unwarranted beef because we love ourselves enough to not compromise who we are by*

A CONFIDENT ME

bending down to a level we have surpassed.

Now let's get into value. When we value something, we hold it in high regard. It is precious to us and we want to be sure it is well taken care of.

What are some material things you hold in high regard?

What about your cell phone? If you have a smart phone you probably have a protective case for it and maybe even a screen protector because you want your phone to remain in good condition. You probably charge it up at night so that you can get the best use out of it. If your device is moving slow or acting weird, you may even take the time and close out the applications you're not using or even do a reset to ensure your phone's functionality.

You probably don't even allow certain people to use your phone, right? We all know that person with butter fingers or clumsy feet and we cringe every time they come near our phone because God forbid we end up with a broken phone with a cracked screen like theirs.

We value our beloved cellular devices because we love them. They have become apart of our lives and we want them to maintain their usefulness. Maybe

it's not your phone. Maybe it's shoes, jewelry, a new game, or even an outfit.

Since we take such good care of things we love, shouldn't we be taking good care of ourselves too? After all we do love ourselves now, right?

Now that we see our worth and value, we need to hold ourselves in high regard.

We need to take good care of ourselves, protect ourselves, and ensure we are functioning correctly and maintain usability.

WE ARE VALUABLE. GOD CREATED US with a purpose and it is our responsibility to ensure we maintain and even increase our value.

Now, this isn't done by wearing the latest trends of clothes and shoes, or rocking the best hairstyles. There's nothing wrong with wanting to look nice, but keep in mind, those things are superficial and have nothing to do with your value.

Maintaining and increasing your value requires **self-care**.

In order to function properly and maintain your usefulness, you have to take good care of yourself.

Let's focus on the 'Five F's' to ensure proper care of ourselves.

Forgiveness

Has someone hurt you, embarrassed you, or taken advantage of you?

Going back to our general codes of conduct

we are taught that when someone offends us in someway, forgiveness comes after an apology is offered. Well let me tell you something, there will be plenty of instances in your life where people hurt you (even the ones who love you) and there will be no apology presented. Does that mean we continue to hold a grudge against them never letting go of what they did to us until the day we die? (dramatic, I know) Absolutely NOT.

We have this sort of **innate** rule in us where we believe forgiveness is a gift or a privilege to the person who offended us.

Well if you haven't heard it before, I'll be the first to tell you, it's not.

Would you believe forgiveness is actually a gift to yourself?

Forgiving someone benefits you more than the person who offended you.

"Unforgiving is like drinking poison and expecting the other person to die,"

LET'S THINK ABOUT THAT A SECOND, imagine sitting at a table with the person who offended you. You have a nice tall glass of poison that you willingly gulp down and you sit there staring into the other person's eyes awaiting their demise. Meanwhile, your insides are slowly **deteriorating** and your organs are shutting down one by one.

THAT IS WHAT UNFORGIVING DOES TO US. The person sitting across from you at that table has moved on with their life and you are literally dying inside.

LET IT GO

If someone has hurt you, embarrassed you, 'played' you, or has taken advantage of you, let it go. Forgiveness is a selfish act, a selfish act that requires you to take part in if you are truly going to value yourself.

Who has hurt you?

What are you secretly holding on to?

Addressing these feelings is like closing out those applications on your phone that you're not using because they're draining your battery. Those idle apps are affecting the usability of your device in the same way those idle hurts are affecting your usability as a person and hindering you from reaching your full potential.

Unforgiving can cause bitterness and even sickness. Holding grudges prevents you from being the very best you can be.

Some of you may be dealing with issues that have had a major impact on your life and it may be an intense struggle to forgive the person or people who may have

A CONFIDENT ME

hurt you. Talk to someone about how you feel, vent about it, write about it if you need to, then let the hurt go.

Remember forgiving the person who hurt you is a gift to you and since you love yourself and want to take good care of yourself you want to do whatever it takes to ensure you maintain your value.

Feelings

Another aspect in taking good care of ourselves and valuing ourselves is expressing how we feel. Forgiveness is a huge part of addressing our feelings because we don't want anything holding us back from reaching our full potential. We want to get into the habit of expressing our feelings in general. Now, I'm not saying express all of your opinions about other people because that wouldn't be helpful or kind and remember kindness is apart of who we are now, but expressing our feelings, when someone has hurt us or we feel misunderstood allows us to function better. Releasing those things allows us to function better.

IN OUR 'KINDNESS & CONFLICT' chapter, we discussed how in a conflict people want to be heard. Well, people can't hear you if you are not saying anything. Expressing our feelings can help us solve conflict. When you say how you feel you also have the opportunity to squash problems before they arise.

When we express our feelings, we hold people accountable for treating us well. When someone says or does something we don't like, or rubbed us the wrong way, addressing it gives them the opportunity to treat us the way we want and deserve to be treated. They start to understand how we want to be loved and cared for when we tell them how we feel.

Failing to express our feelings will leave us feeling unhappy in relationships of all kinds because we never expressed what we wanted or how we felt about things.

We will even find ourselves being unhappy in life because we weren't honest with ourselves about what we wanted.

If we are to live out our full potential, walk in our purpose and maintain and increase our value, it is important for us to be happy. In order for us to be happy we need to be expressing how we feel, not bottling our feelings up.

Our feelings matter and we owe it to ourselves to express how we feel.

HAVING A HEALTHY MIND REQUIRES expressing our feelings even when we don't want to. If you are challenged with expressing your feelings, reach out to a counselor or another adult that you trust to give you a safe place to express how you feel.

SIDE NOTE: FEELINGS MAY BE IN OUR

Five F's but you'll spot feelings in each of our categories.

Fuel

Much like your phone needs to be charged to get its best use and a car needs gasoline, you too need fuel to be at your best. You need fuel to maintain and increase you value and function properly.

Our 'fuel' comes in different ways. Food, of course is an important fuel for us. We want to eat the right foods that increase our energy like bananas, strawberries, spinach, Greek yogurt. We also want to eat our junk food and artificial sugars in moderation because we want to be healthy and live long.

We want to drink plenty of water because doing so will also increase our energy and boost our **metabolism**. Drinking lots of water also helps our skin to glow and our hair to shine.

You know what else is fuel?

Physical activity. Living up to our full potential requires pushing our body beyond its limits. Maybe you're athletic and you play a sport so you are constantly pushing your body and staying active. Maybe sports aren't really your thing, that doesn't mean you shouldn't find some sort of physical activity that gets your heart pumping. Engaging in a physical activity can strengthen your heart and muscles, it can help boost your mood, and even help you sleep better at night. When it comes to holding yourself in high regard, you have full control! It's all about making good decisions even when it's hard.

THE THINGS YOU WATCH AND LISTEN TO also contribute to your fuel. Be mindful of what you watch on TV or social media, or what you listen to. Pay attention to the way those things make you feel (feelings again) and react. Those things are contributing to how you function and you don't want anything affecting your usability or functionality.

Fun

What are you good at?

I ask this question because we usually have fun doing the things we are good at. If we are to maintain and increase our value, we need to have fun! Not just any kind of fun, fun doing the things we enjoy.

In our 'Self-Love' chapter the question asked was, "what are you good at?" If we are to get the full use out of ourselves and walk in our purpose, we need to find the things we are good at and strive to get better at them.

When God made you, He made you with a purpose. Every part of you was intentional. No mistakes, none. Every part of you makes up your purpose. If you want to find your purpose, start by thinking about the things you are naturally good at and strive to be better at them. No better way to hold ourselves in high regard than finding our talents, perfecting them and using them to propel us and help others.

What do you enjoy?

What are you good at?

What are you going to do to get better at that thing?

Friends

We may think a friend is just someone we spend time with, or talk on the phone to, or text. Maybe someone who makes us laugh and we have a good time with. All of those things are cool and we should be able to laugh and spend good time with our friends. But who are your friends for real?

A friend, a companion, is someone whom you share a mutual bond with meaning they feel the same way about you that you feel about them. Someone who encourages you, defends you, someone who supports you.

In the same way we limit our phone access to certain people, we should be limiting access to ourselves to certain people.

How do the people you call your friends treat you?

How do they make you feel? (feelings again)

Can you trust them?

Can you depend on them?

The people you call your friends should make you a better person. You shouldn't feel bad about the decisions you make while you are with your friends because you shouldn't have to compromise who you are. You know what else? They shouldn't make you feel bad about who you are and who you have committed to being.

. . .

It's not easy to end a friendship or keep a distance from people who don't mean us well, but because we love ourselves and value ourselves, we need to protect ourselves.

Limiting access to certain people also helps us in setting ourselves apart. If we are going to stand true to who we are, it is **imperative** (very important) that we distance ourselves from people who go against that standard.

Notice how the word 'feeling' frequently came up. Honestly, when you value yourself you feel good inside! Which means you should steer clear of things (and people) that make you feel less than or uneasy.

Loving yourself feels good so taking care of yourself should feel good too!

Recap:

- You are valuable!
- We take good care of the things we love so it's no wonder we need to take care of ourselves
- Feel, forgive and let go
- Remember your Five F's

NOTES

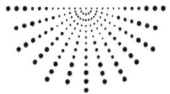

GLOSSARY

Alienation: To be isolated.

Aspect: A particular part of something.

Compassion: To be able to show sympathy or concern; to be kind.

Conflict: A dispute, disagreement or misunderstanding.

Deteriorating: To get increasingly worse.

Ella Baker: Black American woman who helped organize the Southern Christian Leadership Conference (SCLC), also ran

GLOSSARY

voter registration for Crusade for Citizenship.

Empathy: To understand someone else's feelings; to be kind.

Encouragement: To give support or confidence to someone; to be kind.

ESV: English Standard Version translation of the Bible.

Exclusion: Set apart; Denied access.

Feelings: An emotional state or a reaction.

Flo Jo: Florence Delores Griffith Joyner, a black American track star; considered the fastest woman of all time.

Friends: Companions, people whom you share a mutual bond.

Friendliness: To be friendly, warm, or welcoming; to be kind.

Forgiveness: To pardon, acquit, or clear.

Fuel: To supply or give power.

GLOSSARY

Fun: To enjoy or find pleasure in something.

Generosity: To give in abundance; to be kind.

Grueling: Hard, requiring much effort.

Imperative: Very important; crucial.

Indentured Servants: An employee who is obligated to a contract for a set amount of time.

Innate: Already existing; inborn.

Kindness: The act of being friendly, encouraging, considerate, and loving.

Loyal: To support or be committed to; to be kind.

Marva Collins: Black American teacher, In 1975 Started the Westside Preparatory School in a low income neighborhood in Chicago called Garfield Park.

Metabolism: The process of your body

converting what you eat and drink into energy.

NLT: New Living Translation version of the Bible.

Parched: Dry because of intense heat.

Patience: To be able to accept a delay without being upset; to be kind.

Prevalent: Widespread; common.

Projection: The presentation of an image on a movie screen.

Projector: A visual device that projects an image onto a screen.

Self-care: To have care and concern for one's own self.

Self-love: The celebration and appreciation of one's self.

Self-worth: Confidence in one's own abilities; pride, self-esteem.

Status Quo: The standard opinion.

Stereotypes: A general common set of opinions of a person or group of people.

Thoughtfulness: To consider the needs of others; to be kind.

Transatlantic Slave Trade: The process of slave traders taking Africans from West African countries to the Caribbean and the Americas to enslave them.

Value: To hold something in high regard; the importance or worth of something.

Workmanship: The quality of how something is made.

Zora Neale Hurston: Black American author of *Their Eyes Were Watching God*, *How it Feels to Be Colored Me*, *Every Tongue Got to Confess*, and others.

ABOUT THE AUTHOR

Melodie Williams is a graduate of Southern Illinois University where she studied Journalism and Marketing.

Having a passion for encouraging young black girls, she started Melanin Harmony in 2016, a company committed to promoting self-love and love for one another among young girls of color.

Melanin Harmony's first mission was to

combat 'colorism' in the black community by creating 'Love Your Melanin' and 'Respect Her Melanin' apparel for women and girls of all ages.

Melodie's mission and purpose is to continue to instill confidence in young black girls through books, products, film, and forums.

facebook.com/MelaninHarmony
instagram.com/MelaninHarmony